VULNERABLE SUPPLICANT

DAVID BARTON

Published by the author with the assistance of an award from The Arts Council of Great Britain.

ISBN 0 9505907 0 3

For my teacher, Anton Ehrenzweig,
27th November 1908
5th December 1966

At the beginning of this book, I have described with words, the various transformations which occur in my drawings. As the work progresses however, the text becomes also an independent means of expression, not just a straightforward explanation of the drawings. The drawings in turn, become more explicit and less dependant on verbal support.

There is no conclusion, the book simply stops at a point where a group of drawings have reached a particularly definite stage, and before they resume their process of decomposition and transformation into another aspect of themselves.

RIDDLE

I don't decide what to say
I don't know what to say
But what I do say, I mean.
(Although I don't know what I mean
Until I have said it.)
Often I mean what I say without knowing
What I mean,
And just as often I mean what I say, because
I don't say what I mean.

I would be prodigal; continually concerned with the act of self waste. Repeatedly destroyed as an act of faith upon the lap of the Belly of Infinite Promise.
(Drawing is tangling space) DRAWING IS *UN*TANGLING SPACE.
I am caught within a circle of making which contains—excludes all else.
I AM AT THE END AND AT THE BEGINNING
I AM NOT WORKING 'TOWARDS'
I AM WORKING
WORK IS NOW
      IS THE SAME ALWAYS
TO HAVE DONE IS THE SAME AS
NOT TO HAVE DONE
REALITY ONLY EXISTS AT THE POINT
OF DOING.
All I learn from experience is that I learn nothing from experience.
Reality can only exist in the act now.
One cannot *get rich* in reality. One cannot accumulate it in order to enjoy it. It can only be felt in the act of making *now*. Yesterday's reality is already dead.

INTRODUCTION

The following pages have been selected from almost two hundred notebooks, which have constituted the main body of my work over the past twelve years. (Sept.1964—July 1976)

I began to keep a record of my search for ideas, in 1964 on the advice and with the encouragement and help of Anton Ehrenzweig, who was at that time a Lecturer on the Art Teachers Certificate course at Goldsmiths College. Four of my drawings are reproduced in his last book, *The Hidden Order Of Art*, published by Weidenfeld and Nicolson.

Originally these notes were a testing ground for themes which were later carried out in large paintings and three-dimensional constructions.

Very quickly however, this initial process of wrestling with the content of my work in words, drawings, and watercolour paintings, began to demand all my time.

The need to attempt larger, more time-consuming pieces was eventually quelled by the urgency of my day to day search.

I became certain of a growing conviction that a complete involvement in, and investigation of, my working process over an indefinite period of time would be the most thorough way of clarifying my imagery; each new growth being related to, dependent on, and justified by the family tree from which it continually springs.

Therefore the task which obsesses me is that of keeping a diary of events in my daily struggle to remain in contact with and understand more clearly, that reality which is the motivation and content of my work. It is a diary of my life, the events of which are created by and contained within the work which expresses them.

It is a diary concerned with the creation of myself.
Through it, I am made daily.
Expelled from it, I am lost.
Nothing else matters except this diary,
Because nothing else happens.
Nothing else happens except this diary,
Because nothing else matters.

Bearing in mind that a great many water colour paintings which are an integral part of my search, have necessarily been omitted, as well as much of my drawing and writing, and that many pieces of work are out of strict chronological order; I have nevertheless tried to give as clear an idea as possible of the way in which my ideas have developed.

VULNERABLE SUPPLICANT

I experienced an initial difficulty. I sensed an image, but I was unable to approach it, except with words. Since this time I have continued to use words whenever I have felt them to be necessary.

Two images which appeared in this first onslaught of words, have remained constant regardless of the forms which they have taken at any particular time.

These are, 1. The Male Figure,
       VULNERABLE SUPPLICANT

and   2. The Female Torso,
       BELLY OF INFINITE PROMISE

While working on an exercise in which cuts were to be made into equi-lateral triangles, I noticed a particular relationship between two of the images.

1.   2.

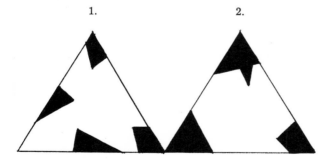

Two triangles from the Exercise.
Although they have details in common, they are complimentary. They look right together, and emphasize each other's qualities.

The implied energy of Triangle 1 is internal. It is only a shadow of what it should be, and requires an understanding of what happens inside, at the centre and source of its energy. This is obviously connected with the perspective lines implied by its outline. It is a Feeler, Describer, or Explorer of the space around itself.

The implied energy of Triangle 2 is external. The centre is void, passive space. The energy has already moved outwards from its centre, and is concentrated in its outline. It is a Container of space, and will only move in order to envelop more space.

The following is a word plan of the two Triangles.

TRIANGLE 1

ASPIRING	CLEAVING	LIBERATED	EXTROVERT	LYRICAL
ENVIOUS	SHEER	SPIRITUAL	VALOUROUS	NOBLE
COVETOUS	INSTRUMENT	DESPISING	BOMBAST	INCISIVE
	COLD	FRAILSTRONG	ANTIC	SWEET
	METAL		VIRTUOSO	SCENTED
	SILVER			
	ETHER			

TRIANGLE 2

ROOTED	CLEFT	STUNTED	INTROVERT	TRAGIC
TAILED	BURST	OPPRESSED	INGROWN	SUPPLICANT
SMUG	BUD	OBSCURE	FLESH	VULNERABLE
STAGNANT	ROTTEN	HERMIT	MORTAL	RAW
SATISFIED	DECOMPOSE	DUMB	MATTED	VEINED
STOMACH	HEAT	QUENCHED	FIBROUS	
CANKER	PARASITE	CORRUPT		
SUBTERRANEAN		REPENTANT		
CAVERN		MARTYR		
PHOSPHORESCENT		SACRIFICE		
MILDEW				
VELVET				
DANK				

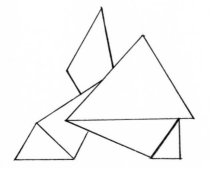
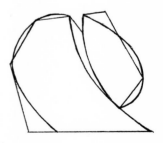

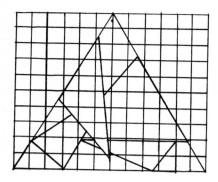 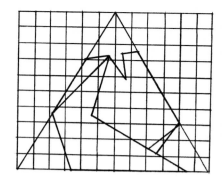

On this page, I have taken the second
Triangle and worked on it, changing and
adding to it in the way suggested by the
word analysis.

ROOTED-STAGNANT-CLEFT-HERMITMARTYR
VULNERABLE SUPPLICANT

A very important part of the image's character
is its rootedness. I worked on this root, which
immediately became a tube, not for taking in
nourishment, but a waste pipe, disposing of the
stagnant rottenness inherent in its characteristics.

It is a hermit, a John the Baptist, entering into
the wilderness, hiding himself inside a deep
cave, purging himself of the collected filth
of existence.

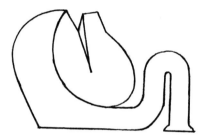

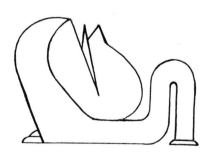

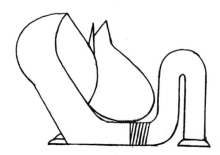

The first drawing shows the root or pipe in conjunction with and around the triangle.

The second drawing is simply the first inverted and altered according to the ideas suggested. It is a shield of hard, polished metal, for the protection of something behind it; the vulnerable martyr is deliberately exposed to barbarity and pageantry.

In the third drawing the martyr is a skull-less soft fleshy head THROTTLED BY ITS ATTACHMENT TO THE SHIELD. The neck moves into a shoulder, upper arm, and ineffectively protective forearm, with a capital in place of a hand, offering something which does not exist.

I MOVED PART OF THE BASE OF THE OBJECT TO A RIGHT ANGLE WITH THE ORIGINAL BASE, AND IT MULTIPLIED INTO THE FINGERS OF THE *HAND*. This hand is not part of the martyr object, but is part of the shield, beaten into the metal. The head is no longer soft, but hard and brittle. Withered upper arm. Large fleshy forearm. PROTECTIVE YET OFFERING — *HARP*.

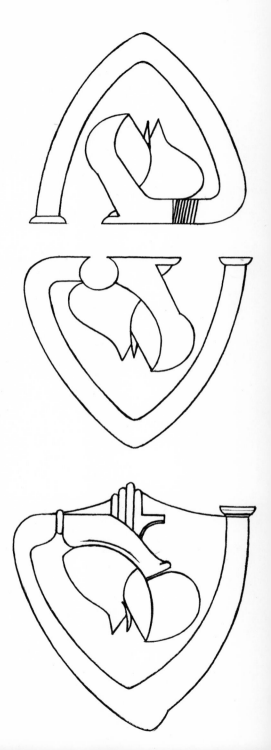

These drawings are an attempt to remake the hermit-martyr of the previous drawings.

The waste pipe is the head. The body is swept over backwards, exposed and vulnerable. The abdomen is taut and full, the rib cage is dry and shrivelled. The legs are dispensable conveniences.

Although the body is completely exposed the martyr has a definite self-confident poise, like a JESTER-ACROBAT.

Although an apparently degraded entertainer, it is oblivious of an audience. IT IS CONVINCED OF A PURPOSE.

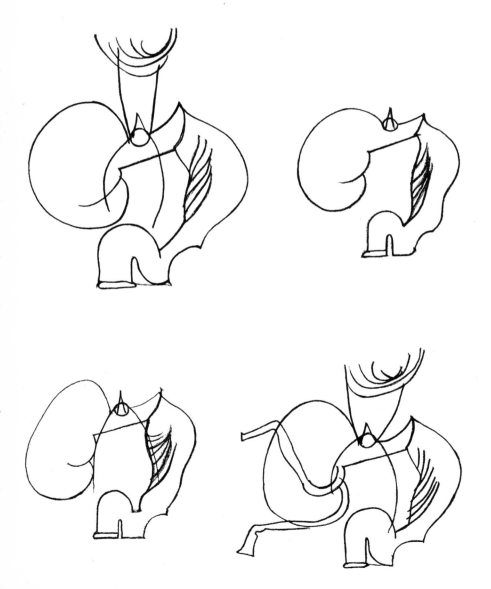

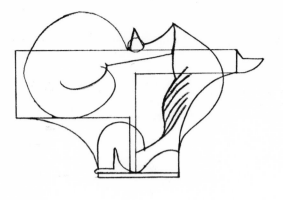

In the first of these drawings I began
by thinking about the palm of the
hand and thumb which is beaten into
the metal of the shield; and the figure
which was the recreation of the
original martyr-supplicant.

The figure is offered, exposed, yet still
balanced and self contained. It has
become locked into the HAND-
ANVIL, and the head has been cast
into the metal at the base or wrist,
(thus supporting the whole.)

In the third drawing I decided to take
away part of the hand in order to
emphasize the delicate balance
between the two sections of the
figure, (thereby making a window.)
It has become a front, show, or
facade.
VULNERABLE SUPPLICANT
JESTER ACROBAT
FACADE

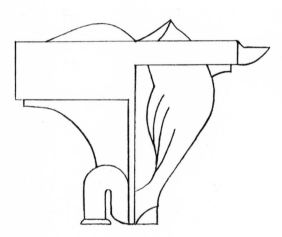

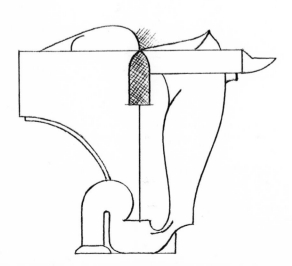

In the drawings which follow, I have used almost the same components as in the previous drawings.

The 'hand facade' is inverted and the figure is now no longer made vulnerable through its immobility, being cast or set into the metal of the anvil, but is bursting upwards and outwards from the shape beneath.

The hand which I used in the shield drawings has disappeared, but has now become far more important again to me because of its resemblance to A TELEPHONE. The figure, like THE RECEIVER, is exposed to the constant threat of being wrenched from its position.

The withered rib cage has disappeared and the navel and throat have become united. The throat is stretched and vulnerable.

The object on which the figure rests is a hard FEMALE TORSO. The head of the figure is soft and pulpy.

In the second and third drawings I have put in the buttons on which the receiver rests.

The dial is the navel of the female torso. It is a hole into the stomach through which the cord is visible which in its turn connects with the navel of the figure above. The fork of the legs is an entrance into the TORSO-CATHEDRAL FACADE. The eyes of the figure are blinded by a layer of skin. The plinth on the left side of the Torso-Facade is a socket. Therefore the Torso-Facade is also the waste pipe.

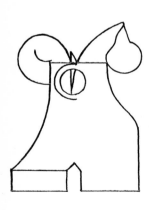

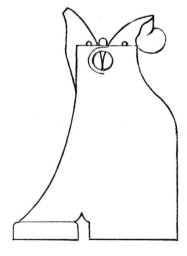

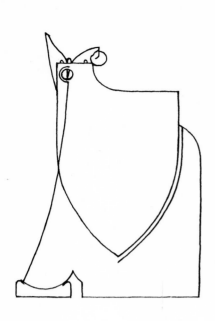

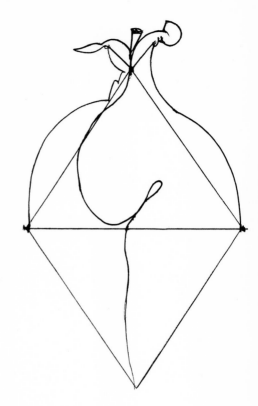

TO THE BELLY

I CANNOT ESCAPE
UNTIL I AM COMPLETELY
FETTERED BY
THE ACTIONS WITH
WHICH I MADE YOU.
I CANNOT BE I
UNTIL I AM YOU.
EVERYTHING BELONGS
TO THE BELLY.
MY WORK IS AN AFFIRMATION.
WHEN I AM NOT WORKING I AM DYING.

DEAD — AN EMPTY BELLY AND AN IRON
LAP.
THE FIGURE IS THE SHOULDERS OF THE
TORSO.
THE TORSO LACKS A HEAD
THE FIGURE LACKS GENITALS

The naked belly and genitals of the torso are
displayed within the triangular opening on the
apex of which the figure is balanced.

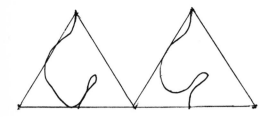

These drawings contain the most important elements of the previous one.

The slack line of the belly hangs outwards from the shallow alcove which contains it.

The triangular thighs are closed.

The shape of the belly is the shape of the head of the figure. The ALCOVE BELLY IS BOTH TORSO AND FIGURE.

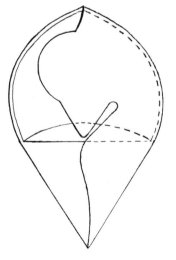

The alcove Belly sends me away from itself. It banishes me from its presence, then calls me back into itself again. I AM SENT ON TRIALS — AND CALLED BACK INTO THE BELLY OF INFINITE PROMISE. The reason for continually returning to the Belly of Infinite Promise— Trickery is that the Belly is like a flower which changes identity on each new opening. On closing it becomes the figure. On opening the figure's identity is changed — the figure is BETRAYED. The loop = eye—sex— crooked-elbow—knee of the torso. It also equals an exploratory splash into the emptiness of the Belly.

Of one thing only am I sure, that is the reality of the Belly of Infinite Promise and Trickery. I must say "Belly of Inifinite Promise" but I must expect only Trickery.

To the Belly-Torso: I MUST BE WILLINGLY TRAPPED. I CANNOT ESCAPE, UNTIL I AM COMPLETELY FETTERED BY THE FORMS WITH WHICH I MAKE YOU. I CANNOT BE I UNTIL I AM YOU.

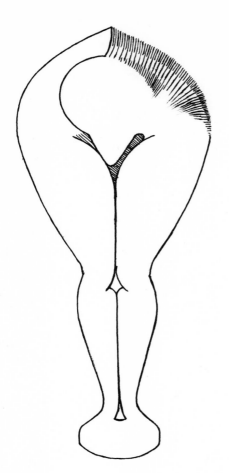

The right side of the dome containing the belly is also a 'mane' — is also a series of spills or splashes.
The Torso pours itself away.

As these drawings continue, each form so readily adopts or assumes its opposite function, that I am no longer able to explain. My conviction about their rightness can only be justified by the inevitability of their development.

The only way in which I can know the Belly, is through submission. I must accept the consequence of being endlessly lost and dissipated in its embrace.

The Belly offers a reconcilement which is death.

I must accept this reconcilement, while finding new ways to press on into the silence and emptiness which is the Belly of Infinite Promise.

THE BELLY, LIKE A CLAM, TRAPS THE FIGURE
THE FIGURE BURSTS INTO IT
THE BELLY IS THE BELLY OF THE FIGURE
                    BELLY OF INFINITE PROMISE.

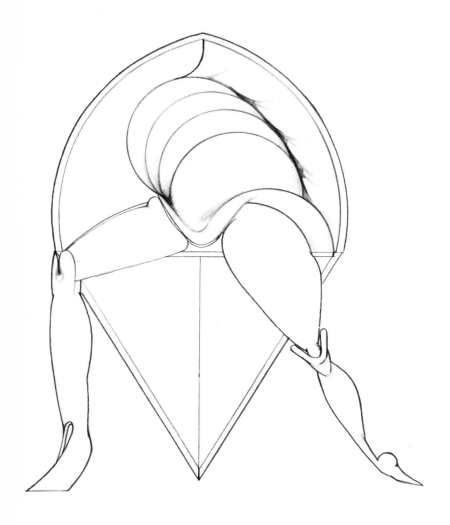

(To be made, like a pressed tin toy, edges strained, stretched, and crumpled.)

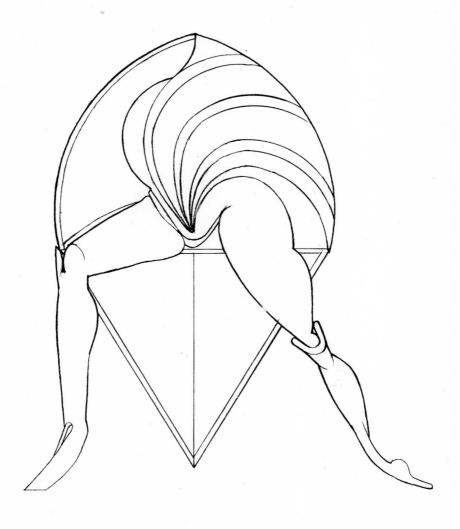

PINCHED IN — LEAVING THE IMPRESSION OF A HAND — KNUCKLES — GLOVE
CURLED LIP — SNARL — LIFTED SKIRT
FOLDED BACK CURTAIN
REVEALING THE THIGHS AND LEGS OF THE TORSO FIGURE

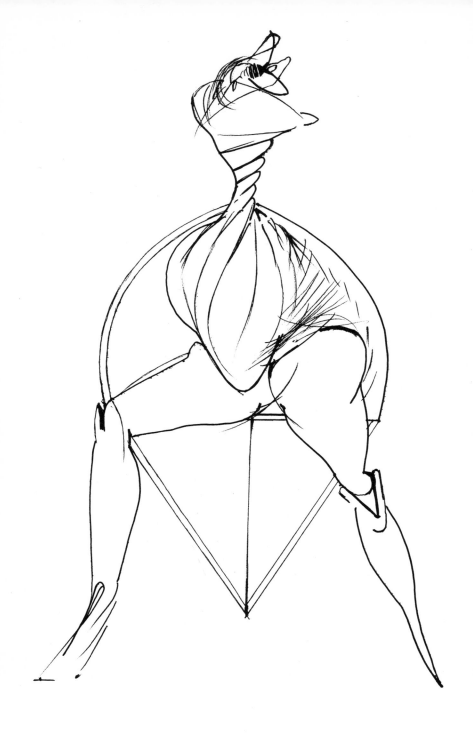

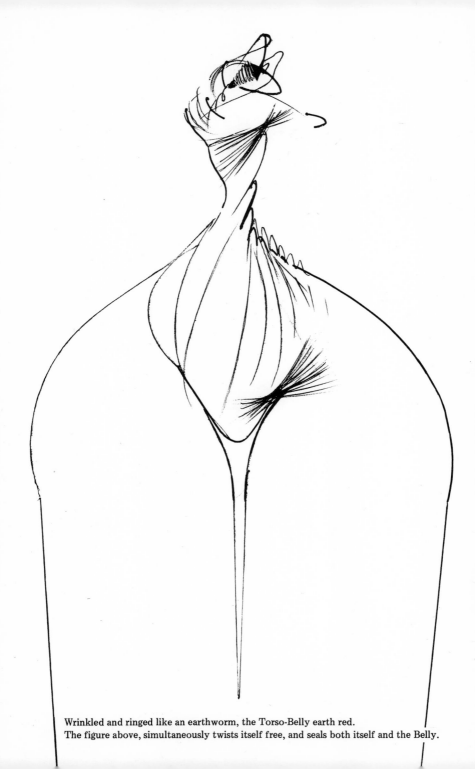

Wrinkled and ringed like an earthworm, the Torso-Belly earth red.
The figure above, simultaneously twists itself free, and seals both itself and the Belly.

I am continually filled with the desire to feel the shape of my life within a drawing, or a sentence, or any piece of work,

Each piece of work is a point of recognition or discovery. A point of identification which is NOW, which is obsolete as soon as known.

DAY AFTER DAY, I REPEAT THE SEARCH WHICH FOUND YOU.
DAY AFTER DAY, I REHEARSE THOSE ACTIONS WHICH BOUND YOU.

DAY AFTER DAY, YOU WEAR OUT THOSE FORMS WHICH SURROUND YOU.

YOU WEAR OUT MY WORK LIKE DISEASE,
IT CANNOT RETAIN YOU;
AND RETURN TO ME WHEN YOU PLEASE.
IT IS I WHO CONTAIN YOU.

WHEN MY SEARCH HAS FOUND YOU,
WHEN MY ACTIONS HAVE MADE YOU,
I REVEL IN THOSE MOTIONS
WHICH SIMULTANEOUSLY MAKE AND TRAP YOU.

BUT THE RISK BECOMES EVER GREATER.
YOUR STRENGTH INCREASES THROUGH IMMUNITY,
AND EACH SUCCESSIVE SHOCK OF YOUR RETURN
DESTROYS MY PURPOSE.

STUNNED, THE SEARCH WHICH FINDS YOU IS A BLIND GROPING.
PARALYSED, THE ACTIONS WHICH MAKE YOU ARE INVOLUNTARY SPASMS.

The now, which is the shape of my life as it is, continually crumbles, leaving only a piece of work as evidence. There is no Before, only a NOW and its Aftermath, and the need to find a perpetual NOW among the ashes of its perpetual Aftermath. There is no respite. My life is and will be always utterly desolate, and myself, perpetually lost, searching for now among the ashes of its own dereliction.

I AM LOOKING FOR SOMETHING WHICH DOES'NT EXIST UNTIL *IT* FINDS *ME*.

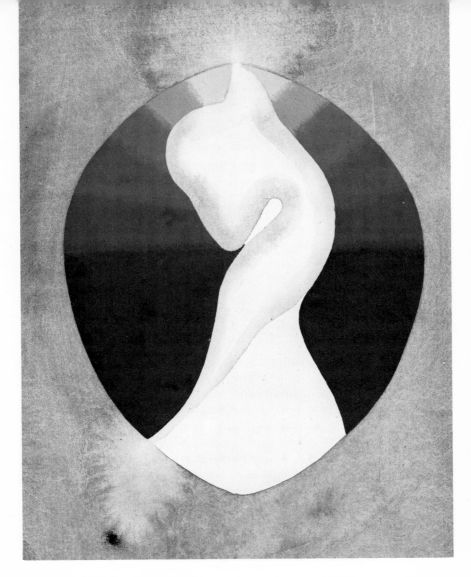

The Belly of Infinite Promise has become the
Figure — suspended within the vessel of
endless wastes.
MOTHER CHILD
CHILD MOTHER
THE BELLY HAS SHRUNK INTO THE FIGURE
BRUISED — COLD.

Regardless of quality, my work is divided
into two streams; one in which I am
'allowed out to play', and the other in
which I am 'called in'.

I have been 'CALLED IN'.

There are times when this 'calling in' is balanced by a physical sense of well-being and
optimism, and there are times when an awareness of death adds a despairing
determination to my desire to 'play out'. There are times when the Belly of Infinite
Promise, promises only Death. The figure which is the shrunken Belly hangs within
the vessel of endless wastes — glows within the vessel of endless wastes.

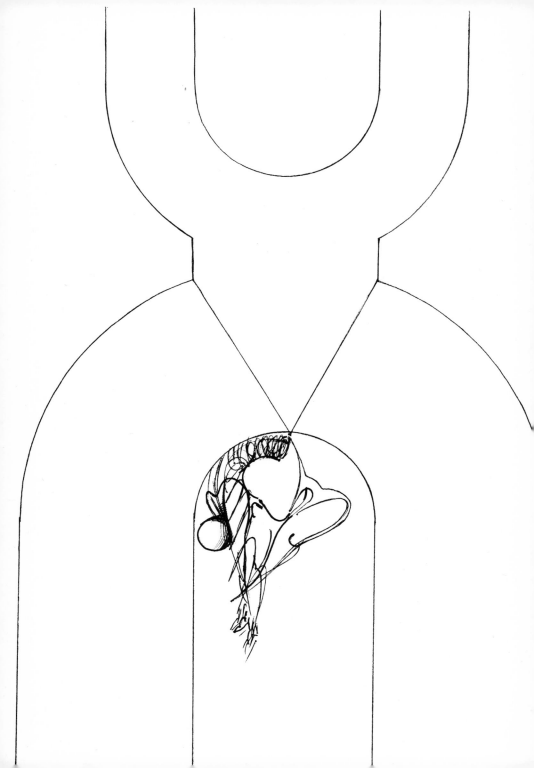

The centre from which everything germinates.
Expands prodigally.
Without reference — without relevance.

THE CENTRE IS THE BELLY WHICH HAS BECOME THE FIGURE
THE MOTHER HAS BECOME THE SON
THE FIGURE WHICH HAS BECOME THE BELLY
THE SON HAS BECOME THE MOTHER.
        Washes of identical grey, which lap against each other and leave deposits which mark the boundaries of the Figure and Torso.
Mixing CURRENTS
      WATERS

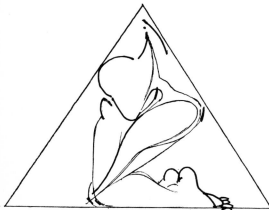

In the drawing which follows, the
crouched figure rises above itse
and leaps from its own belly.
(The Torso has bitten itself a
mouth.)
The figure slithers out of)
         dives from   )
its own belly.
(I am serving a perpetual
apprenticeship of fool's errands.)

The Torso-Figure, like a sower,
sows itself—disjoints itself.
JUGGLES ITSELF OUT OF
JOINT — CASTS ITSELF
AWAY. IT UNDRESSES
     DISCARDS THOSE
FORMS WITH WHICH IT HAS
BEEN MADE VISIBLE. THE
TORSO FIGURE TEARS ITSELF
FREE.

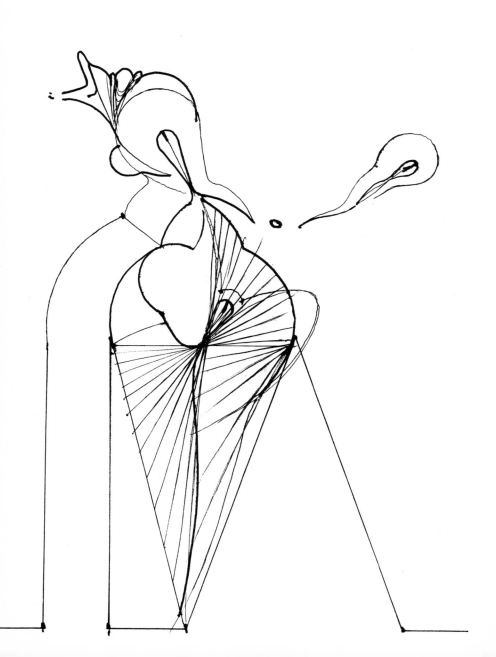

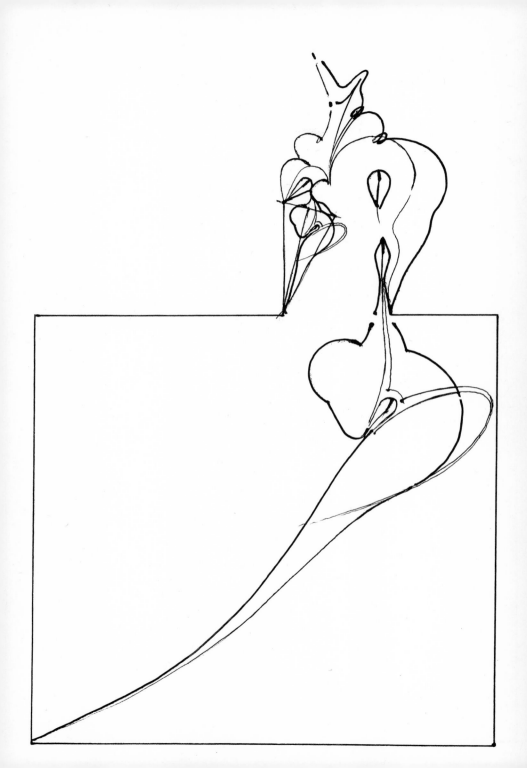

The figure leaps within the torso like a flame in a lamp.

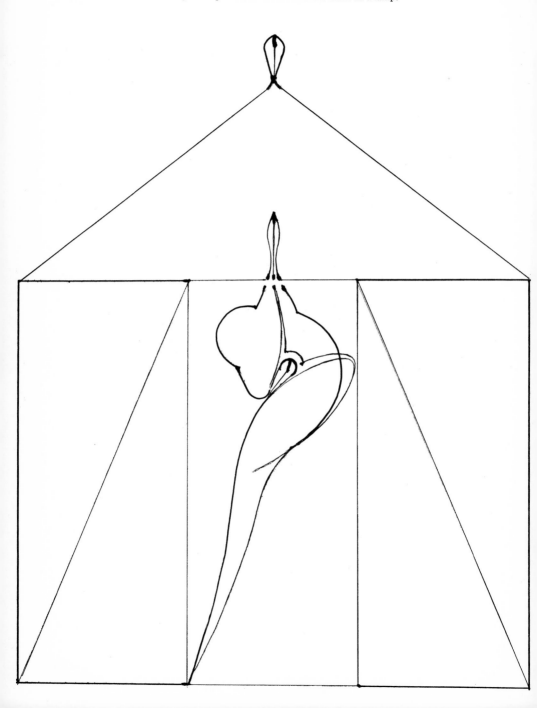

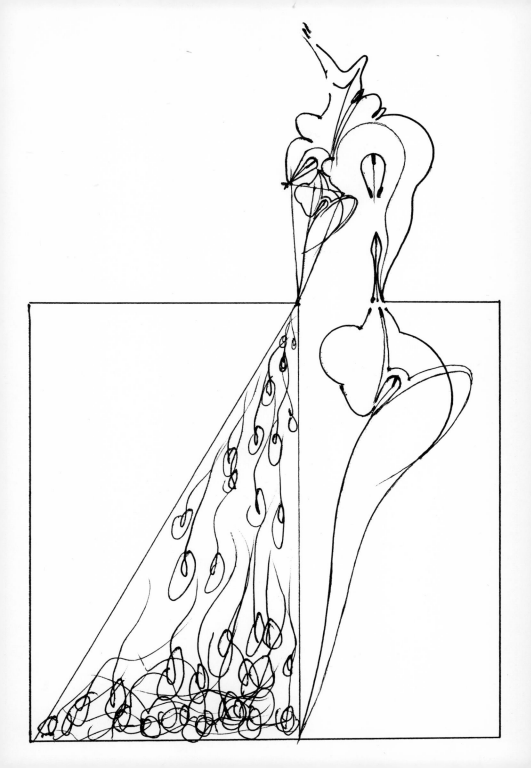

The skirt of the Torso, like a tent, billows outwards, revealing smooth thighs and belly which move about like an inmate or occupant within, separated from the thin ribs and pointed breasts of the upper part.

The Torso advances and swings from side to side, carrying the figure across and as part of, its shoulders and arms.

The Torso cocks an eye (the sidelong glance). The upper and lower parts of the Torso are separated by a semi circular gap. The sides of the Thorax, from hip to underarm, are like the taut muscles of a neck.

In work I must take what is given to me. I lack the sense to choose for myself.

Time carries me towards the point of my birth, not away from it.

Drawings proliferate; each time I attempt to state my position, I continue to alter it.

Each image demands its contradiction.
The figure only demands to be freed in order to waste itself.

I must learn, like the Torso-Figure, to make the 'Side Step'. I must learn the 'Sidelong Glance'. The 'Deliberate Slip'.

In my work, I bring myself to a fruition and extinction, in a rhythm which can never be complete. I am not afraid of the fact that within the Belly of Infinite Promise, fruition and dissolution are the same.

In these drawings, the eyes of the Torso-Figure, like snakes, rise out of the breasts.
Slither down into the breasts.

High cheek bones — Hollow Sockets.

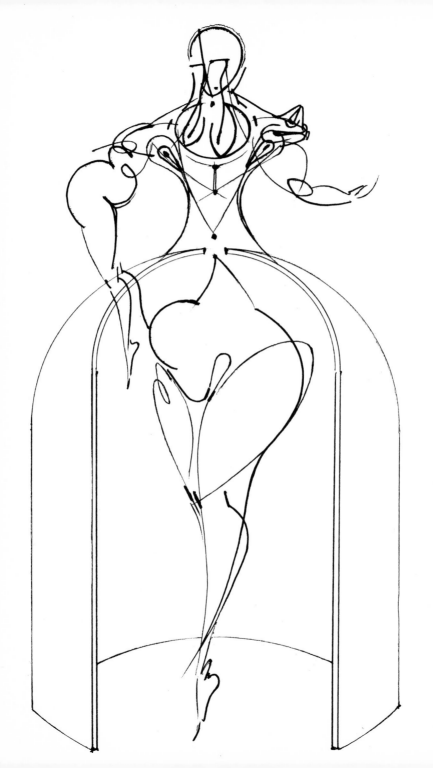

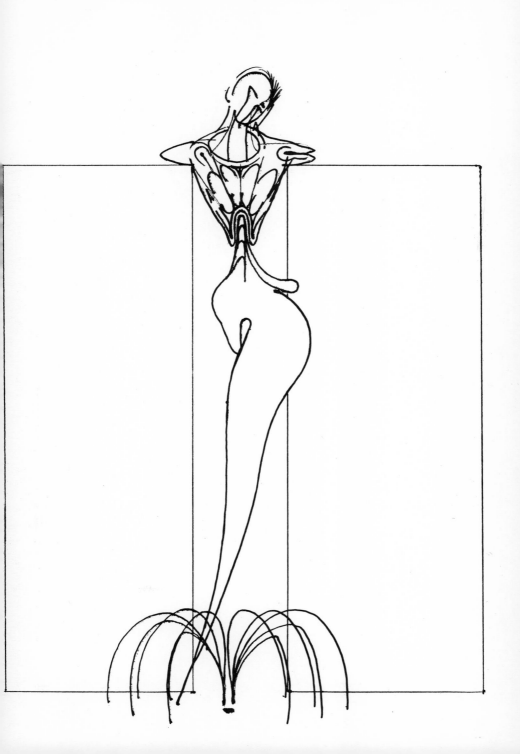

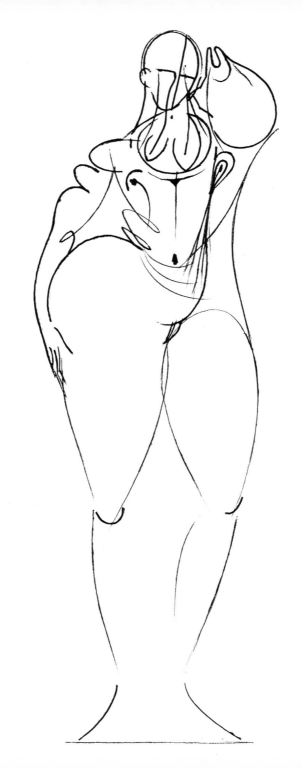

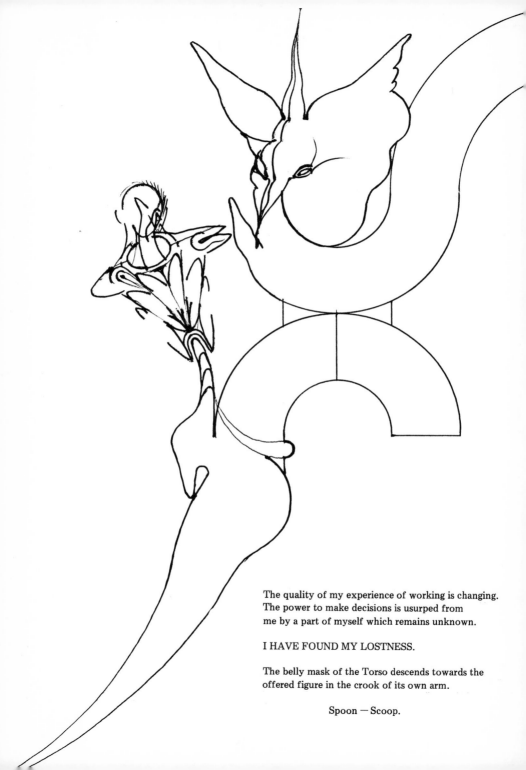

The quality of my experience of working is changing.
The power to make decisions is usurped from
me by a part of myself which remains unknown.

I HAVE FOUND MY LOSTNESS.

The belly mask of the Torso descends towards the
offered figure in the crook of its own arm.

Spoon — Scoop.

The Female Torso Figure displays herself from different viewpoints and in different attitudes. She continues the rhythm of her self contained, self perpetuating existence.

Is offered by herself to herself.

Plunges into, and is buried within her own bowels,
Rises, and balances precariously on her own thighs,
Expands in gestures of self giving,
Contracts upon herself in arcs of despair,
Her face is sucked downwards into her own body,
And emerges watching slyly,
From the wrinkles of her own belly and thighs.
Reality is lost in the very moment of realisation,
Leaving behind only the handle with which it was grasped, the work.

I used to dismiss the recurrence of experiences which I originally felt in childhood, because I believed that their reality lay in the act of recognition of something from the past. Now I believe differently. The reality of those childhood experiences was grasped by me in the same way then as now. The experience was the same when I had no past.

My experiences then, were a realisation of the present and they are now a realisation of that same unchanged present.

It is as if I am working from a store of infinitely subtle glances and expressions. Little slivers of faces, which have slipped into me unawares. Glances so subtle that I did not even know that I had sensed them. Glimpses of expressions just visible beyond flat precipitous cheeks as heads are turned away. I have appropriated them unawares, absorbed them, swallowed them automatically, without taste. I spend my life trying out and fitting these little accidental slivers, these peeled corners of faces, these not quite anonymous glimpses, dipping my hands into the confusion which has entered me. The slippery mass slithers and glints and shimmers continually with a million flashes of 'almost recognition', as slowly and laboriously, and with many often repeated mistakes, I piece together a likeness of myself.

TOO OFTEN REALITY LIES BURIED UNDER THE DEBRIS OF FUTILE ATTEMPTS TO MAKE IT VISIBLE.

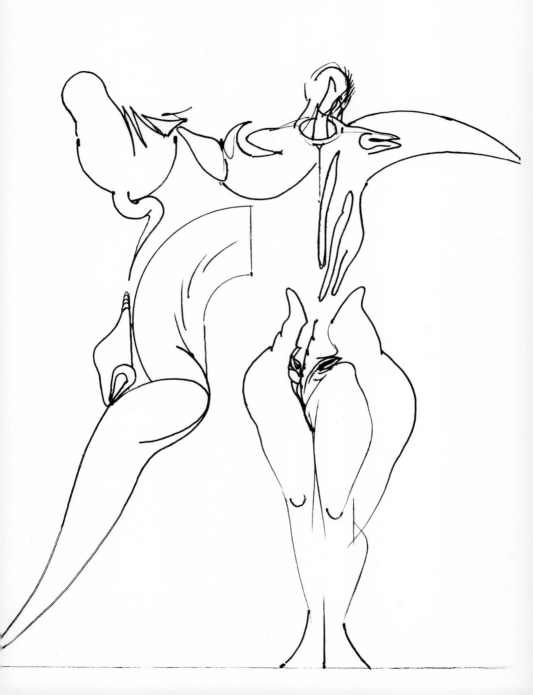

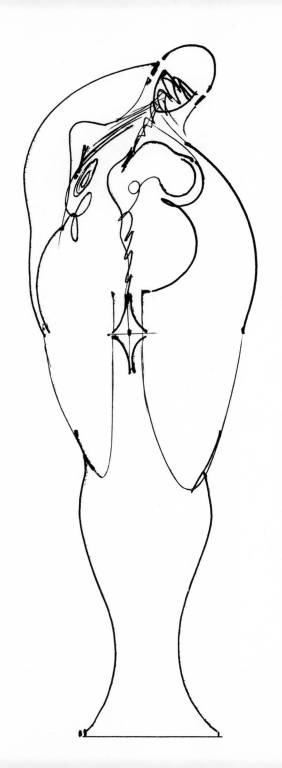

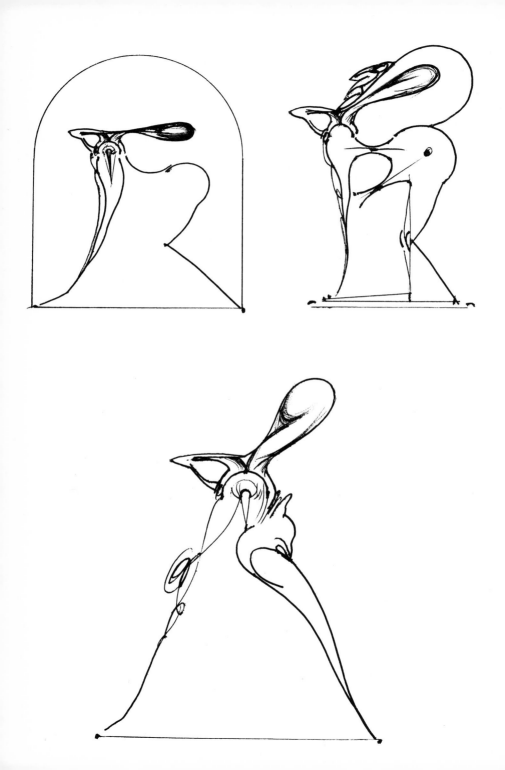

These drawings have reached a maximum tolerance of each other. There is an easy COMMERCE between them. A free interchange of elements, which continue to be relevant — ARE NOT REJECTED.

The DOMED BELLY takes the exhausted figure into itself.
The squint eye of the Torso which is the Breast
                    Crook of the arm of the Torso,⎫
Which is the head of the Figure,
Which is the loop genitals of the Belly of Inifinite Promise.

Like a swimmer, who weaves himself and is woven into the surface of the sea, so I weave myself into and am woven into the surface of my work.

My physical reality is brought about by my work in the same way that my work is brought about by my physical reality.

       When I am drawing I have myself at my own mercy.

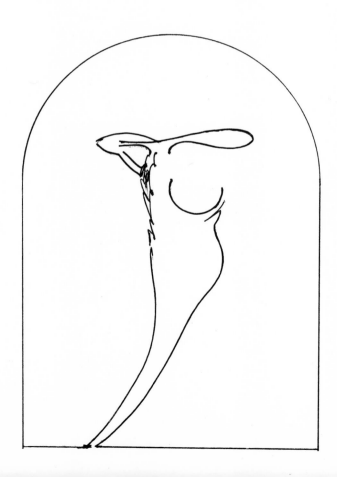

The figure carried by the Torso is now
in duplicate — triplicate.

Has become the fingers of a hand,
reaching upwards into the dome.

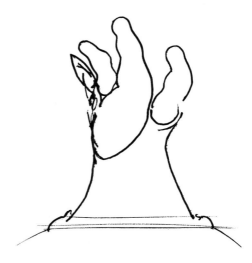

When removed, these figures
        fingers leave an empty socket or vacant seat within the palm of the hand.

A COLLECTION OF TOM THUMBS WHICH REFUSE TO GROW.

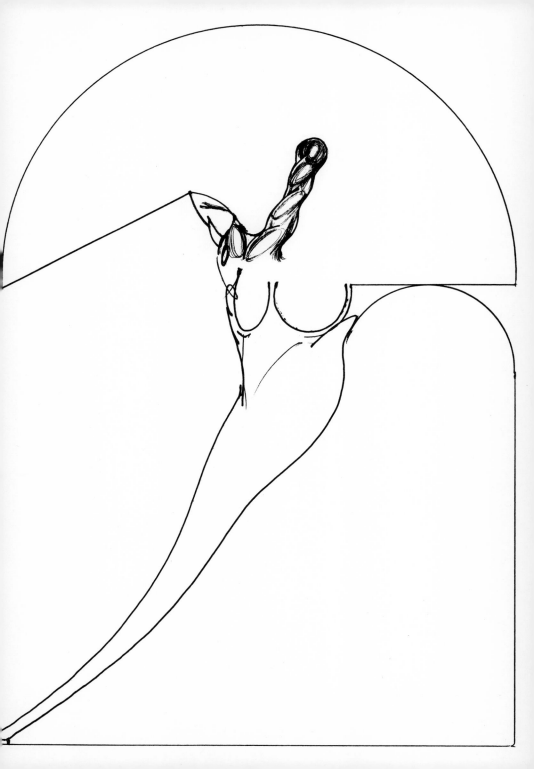

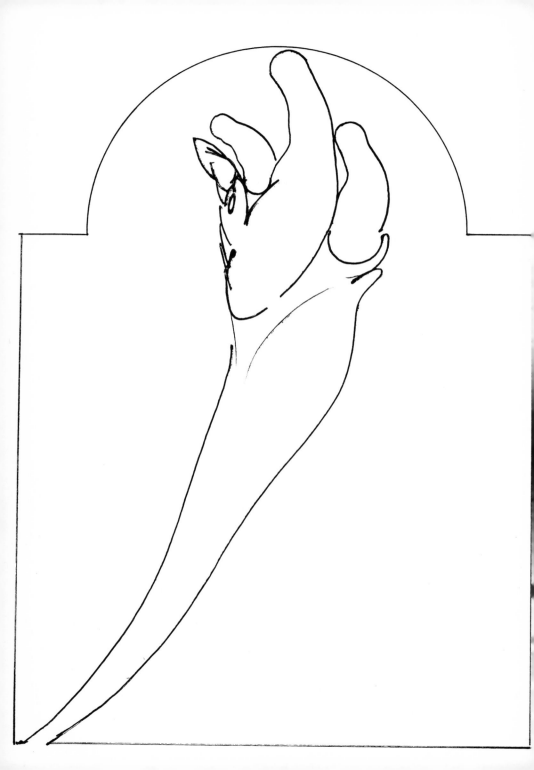

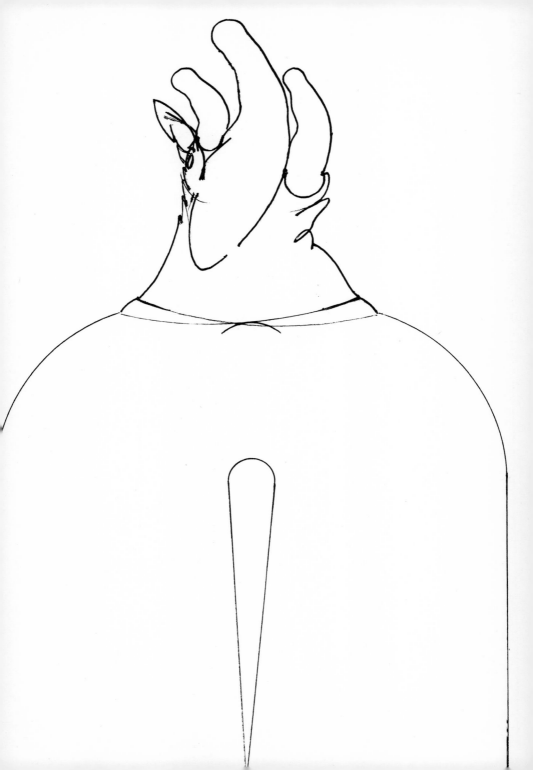

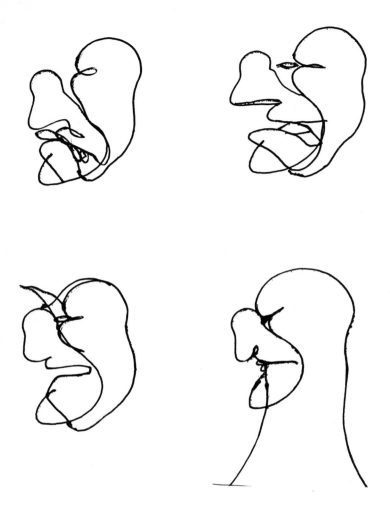

Half moon profile — Toothless face which is the figure. The figure is folded in on itself. THE MOUTH OF THE FACE IS THE FIGURE'S SPLIT BELLY, and the jaw and chin are made by its knees.

In these drawings, the eyes of the face-figure with the double blades $\left.\begin{array}{r}\text{flames}\\\text{wings}\end{array}\right\}$

above and below, leaps to freedom — $\left.\begin{array}{r}\text{divides}\\\text{splits}\end{array}\right\}$ the head-Torso.

The back of the head and jaw, are the crooked arm of the Torso, and the winged eye is the breast.

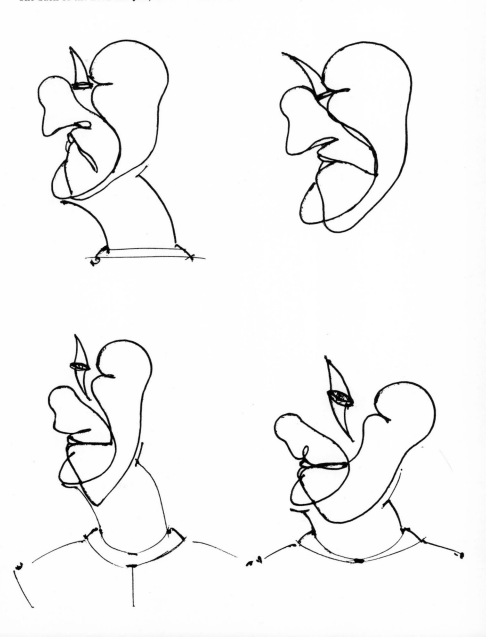

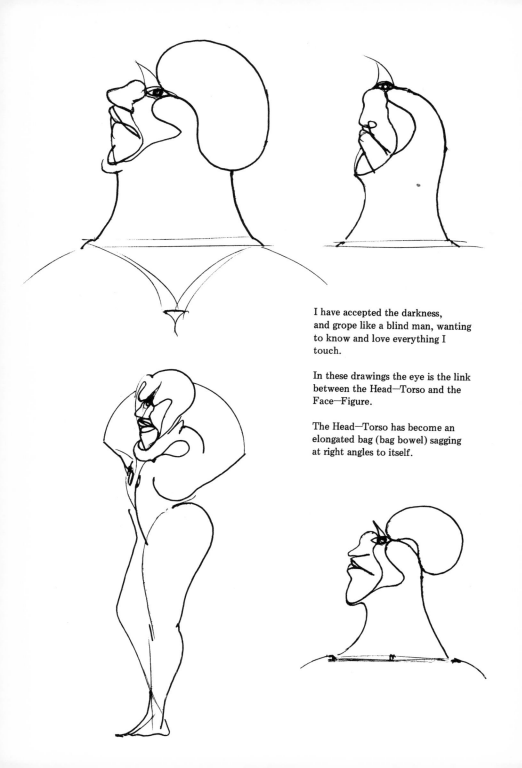

I have accepted the darkness,
and grope like a blind man, wanting
to know and love everything I
touch.

In these drawings the eye is the link
between the Head—Torso and the
Face—Figure.

The Head—Torso has become an
elongated bag (bag bowel) sagging
at right angles to itself.

SMILING WOMAN

The smile on the face of the Female Torso is an obscene leer.
The smile on the face of the Female Torso is the split belly of the Figure.
The toothless, smiling, caved in, wrinkled mouth of the Female Torso, dribbles out the bowels of the Figure.
The genitals of the figure spurt from the smile of the Female Torso.
The eye of the Smiling Woman is little and hard and opaque.
The caved in mouth of the Torso is the caved in belly of the Figure.

PORTRAITS

I am continually working towards a point at which I RECOGNISE that which I have never seen before. To recognise my continual familiarity with that which I am seeing for the first time.

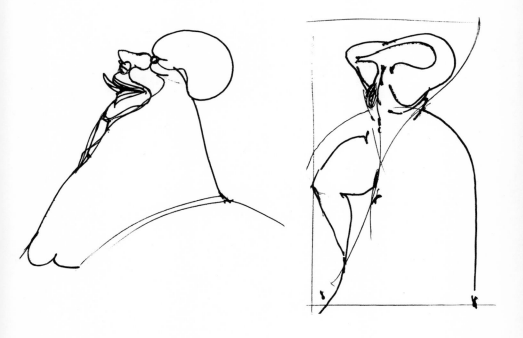

THERE IS ONLY ONE REASON WHY I WORK. I AM AFRAID OF NOT BEING ABLE TO DO THAT WHICH I AM AFRAID OF DOING.

The Cheek is the fulcrum on which the face and head are balanced, at the point where they both meet the eye.

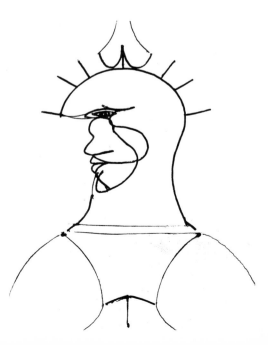

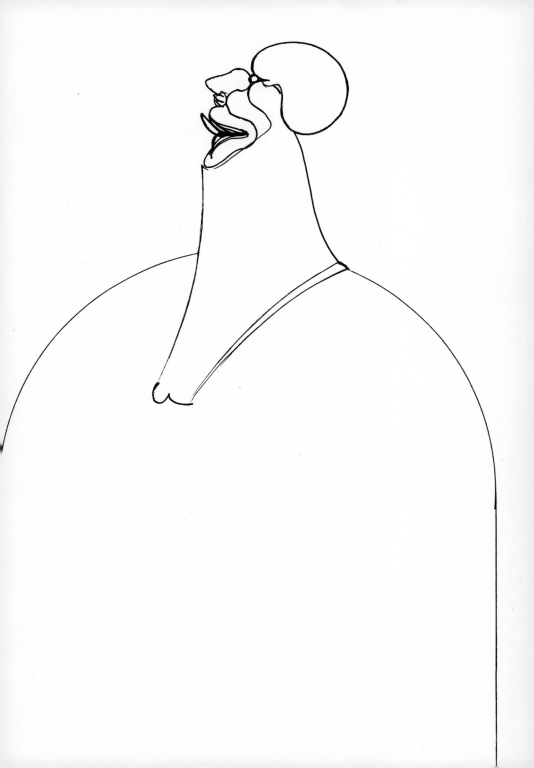

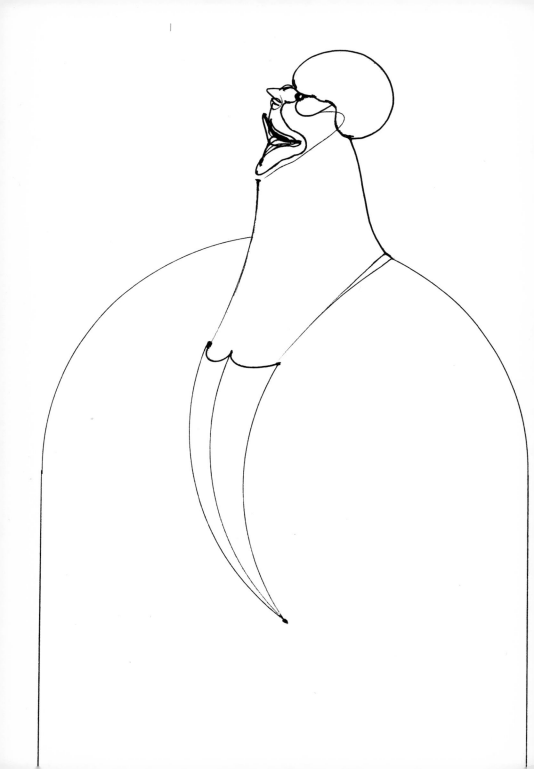

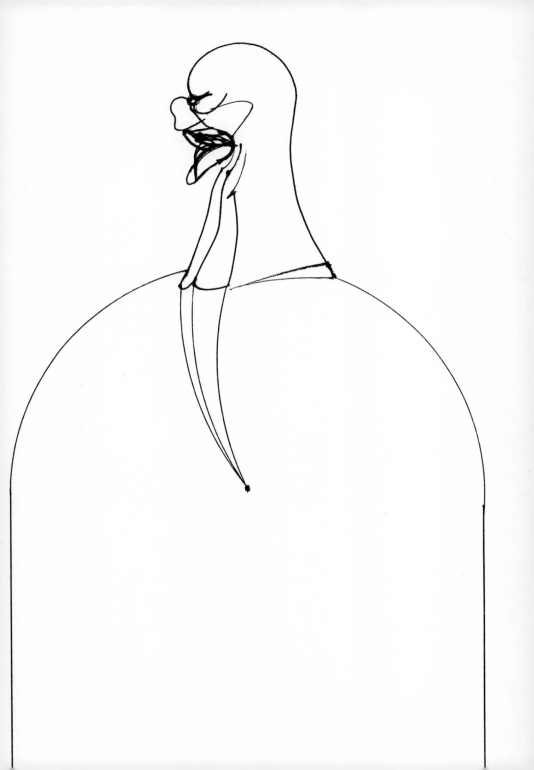

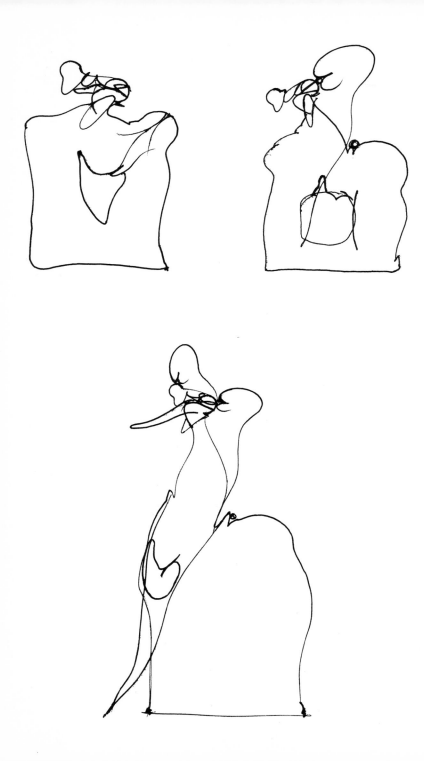

There **is such** an overwhelming chaotic mass which I must try to understand, and only pictures can help me, because they brought it into existence.

I become more and more aware of the fact that as my work establishes contact with reality, it also becomes the very barrier which separates me from it.

DESPAIR when I realise I am taken out of my own hands. When I attempt to touch myself and I am no longer there.

DESPAIR over the makeshift nature of my work. Over the evaporation of reality from the forms with which I work.

DESPAIR at being unable to find the seed of that which I may become within the emptiness of that which I am.

DESPAIR because the reality wears out and evaporates from myself as it wears out and evaporates from the forms with which I work. Because the forms with which I work are mine, and the reality which inhabits them is myself.

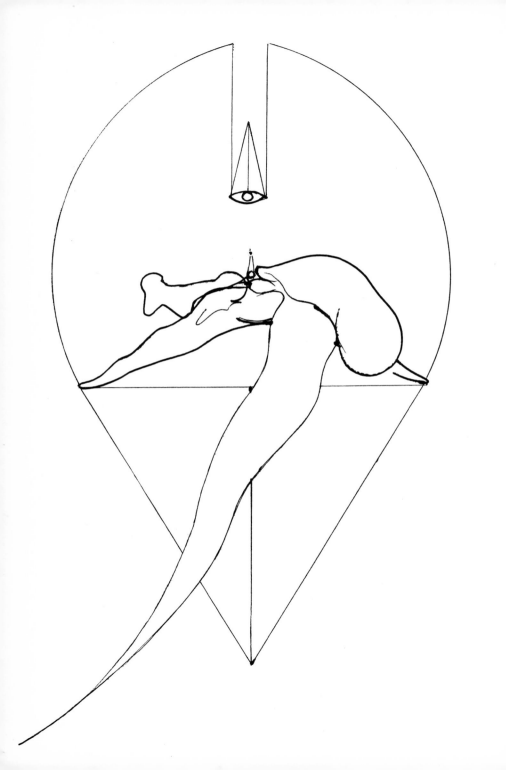

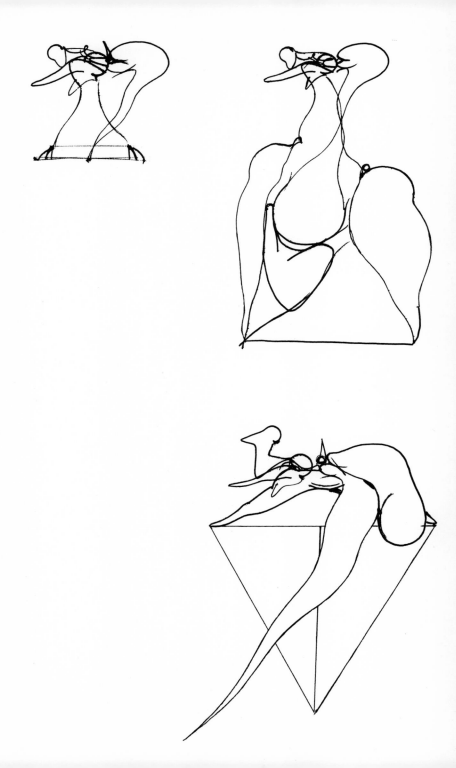

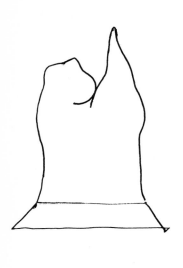

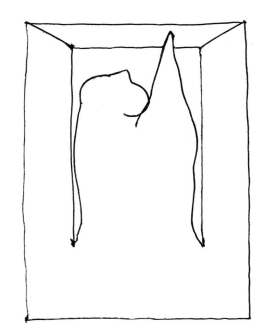

I am working always, in the knowledge that decisions are being continually made without my consent.

I am locked out of myself, kept waiting like a beggar at my own gate, in expectation of those decisions in which I am not allowed to take part.

I am my own stranger.

I admit that I am incapable of those decisions, all I wish is to work.

I will do as I am told.

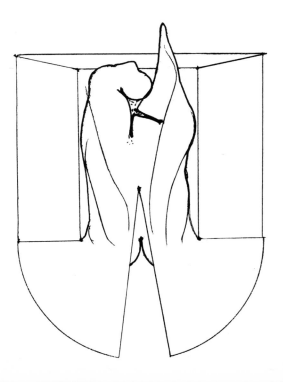

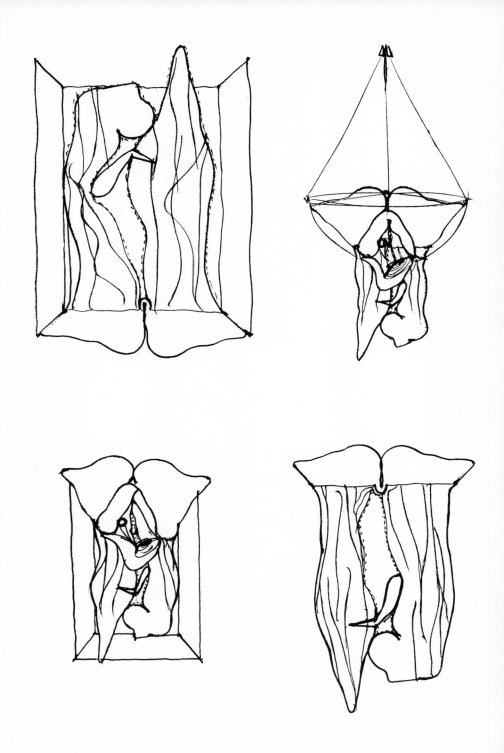

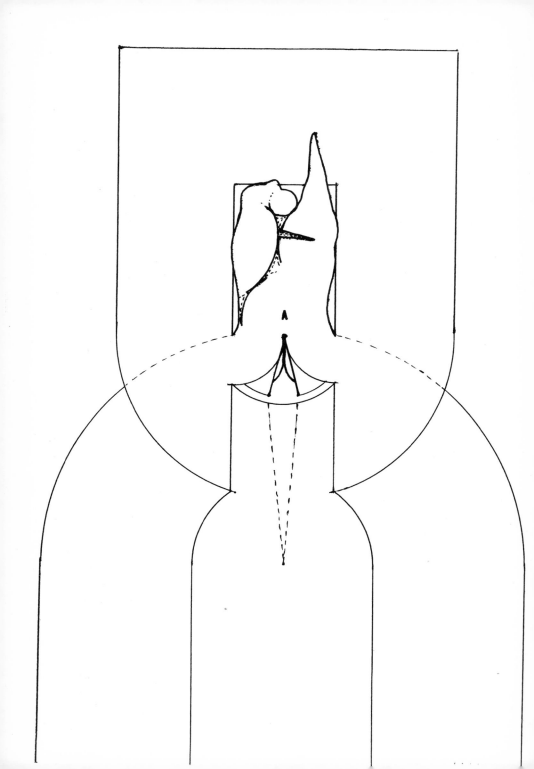

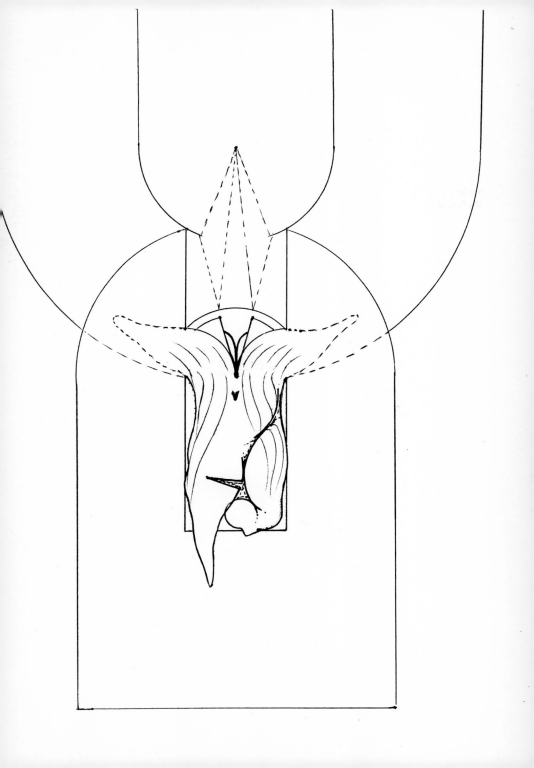

Pay no attention to this false information which has collected around me. Don't expect anything of
me,
We have been deceived.
Ignore the cheap acquisitions which I have ignorantly accepted from childhood, to cover my
nakedness.
I discard them all,
So that I may know the centre around which all these attributes were hung.
So that I may know the magnetic force, which I have only understood through the accumulated
clutter which has succumbed to its attractions, and clusters round the rim of emptiness down which
myself has fallen;
This rubbish, manufactured in order to conceal the fact of my disappearance,
To be a 'stand in', a replacement, possessed of the necessary ability to conceal from himself, myself,
the fact of my absence.

I am not here.

Like a mother leaving her child,
I have said to myself,
'Wait awhile,
Wait and I will come back'.
I am not here.
I am preparing and waiting
For my return.

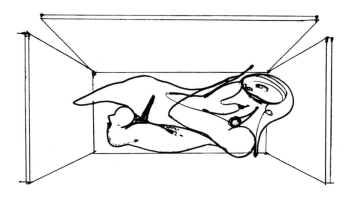

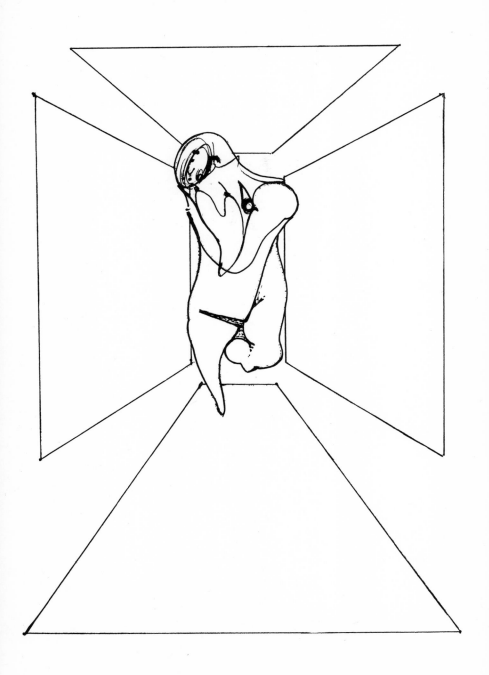

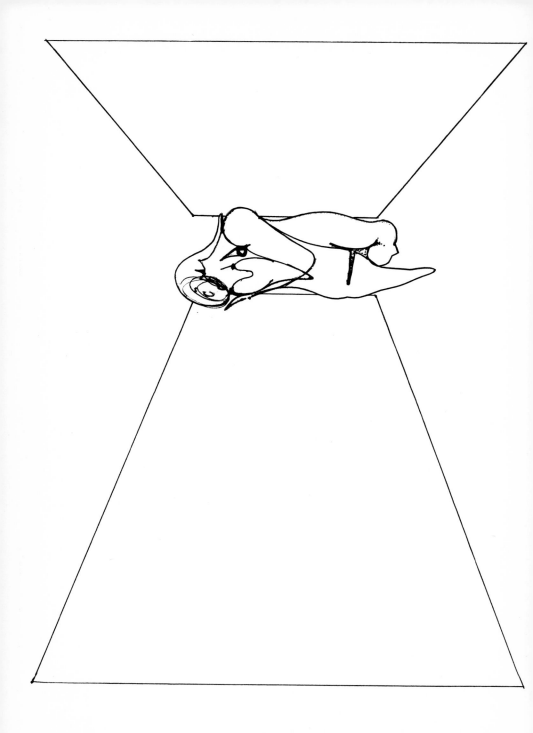

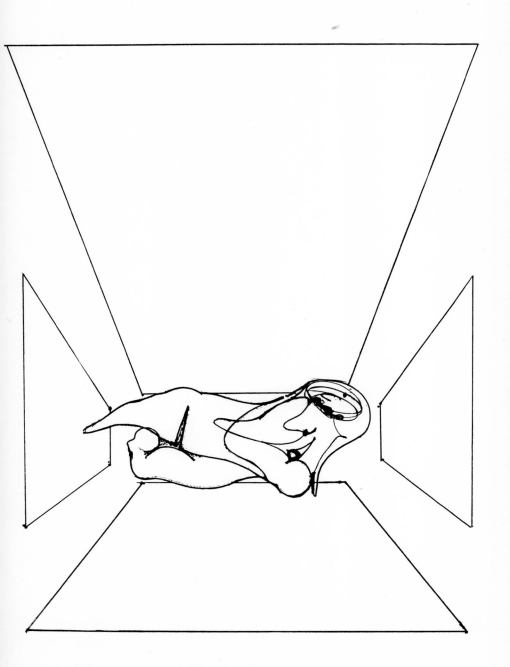

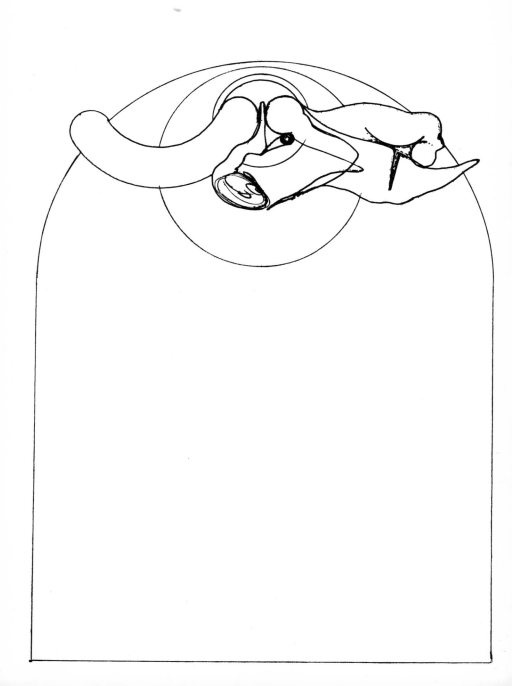

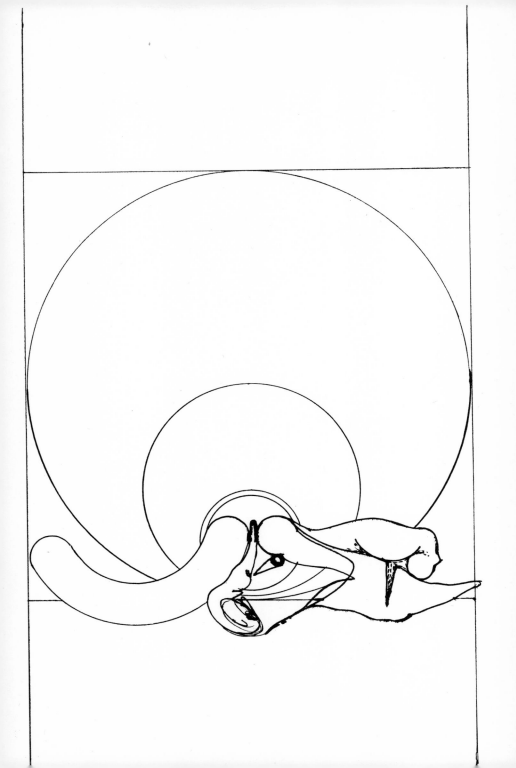

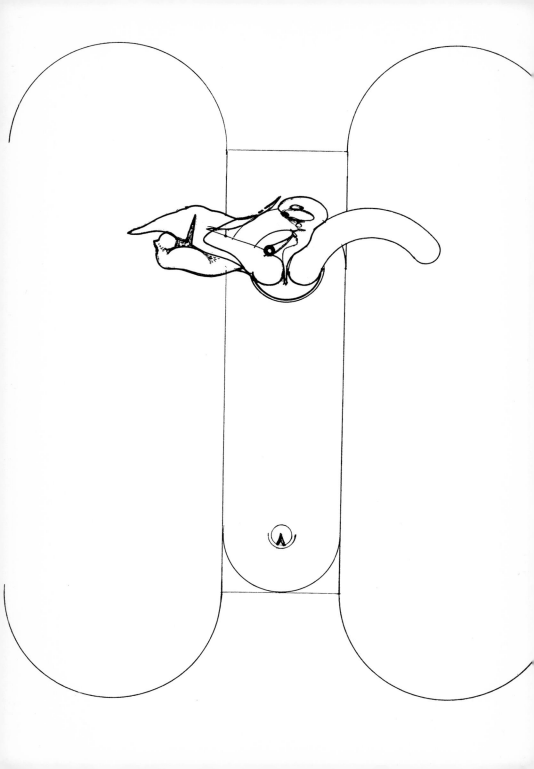

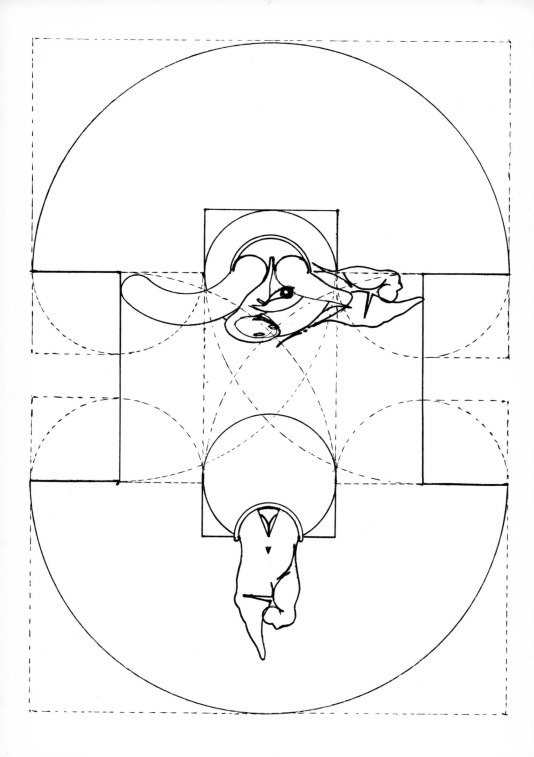

While drawing, it is as if I am reaping something not sown by myself.
Reaping almost mechanically,
Without gratification
Because I must — because I have nothing else.
Because it is my job.
I did not decide to be an artist.
Neither did I set out bravely on a heroic voyage of discovery.
Instead I had to tell myself gently,
In a quiet voice, as one would speak to an invalid,
And the scarcely audible words
Pinned me with a quiet mutilation,
Limp and helpless,
To my beginning.

TORSO TIED IN THE MIDDLE
IN PROFILE
LIPS DRAWN BACK
HALF HEWN TREE
(The wound equals the mouth).
THORAX AND ABDOMEN MEET.

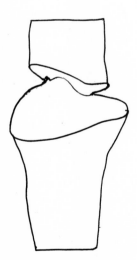
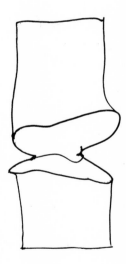

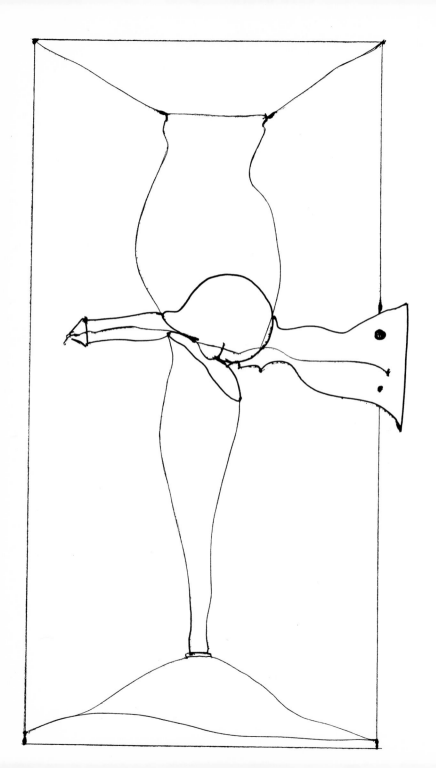

INTERSECTION TO WHICH THE GENITALS ARE FIXED — A flat sheet curled roughly into a tube and GRIPPED at the intersection of vertical and horizontal.

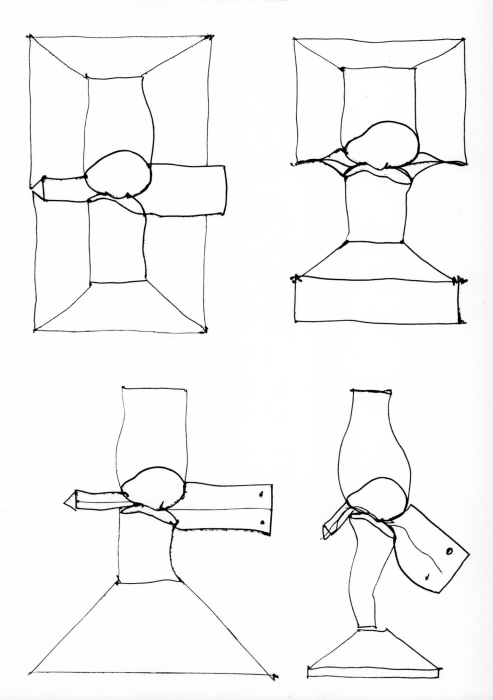

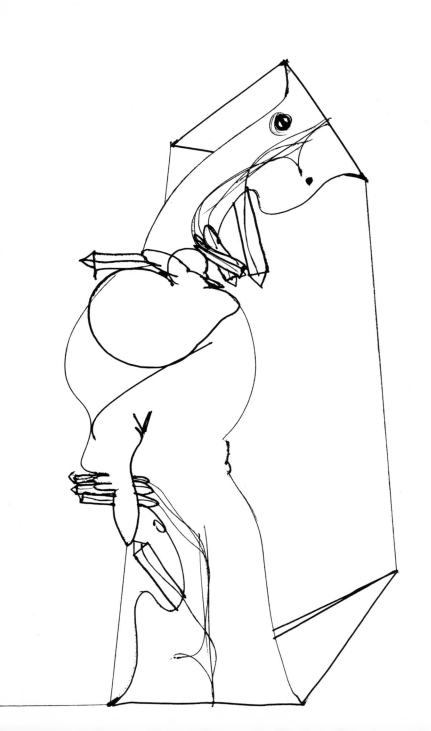

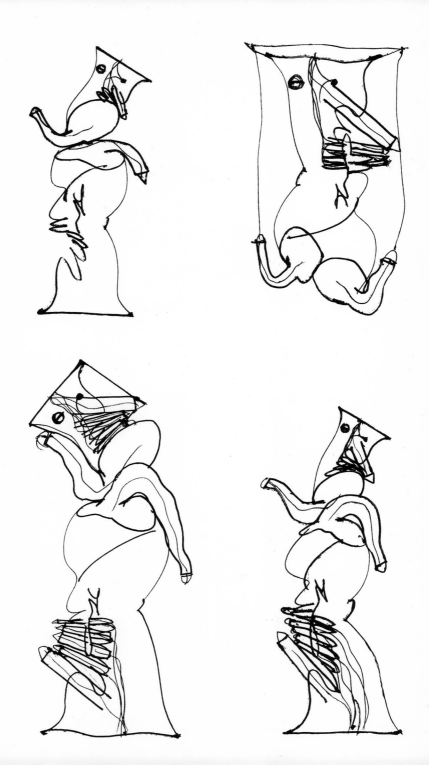

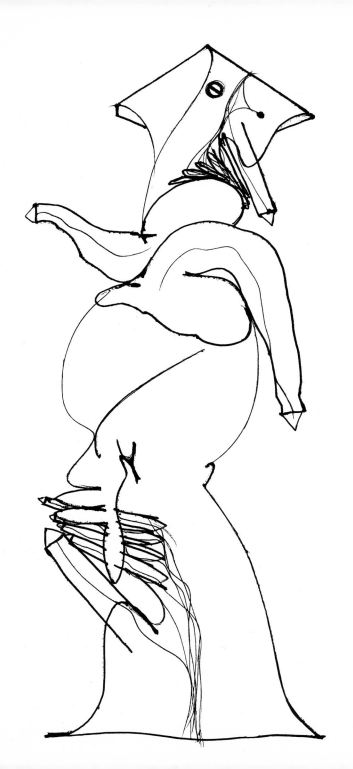

I have no choice in the matter of my work. I simply do what I can. I produce that which I am able to produce. How can I expect more?

I am a magic purse. I put my hand into myself, and find work, the 'currency' which pays for my existence. When I have spent my work, I put my hand into myself again, hoping to find myself once more full of that currency which I need to live.

But sometimes the magic purse is asleep, or damaged, or out of patience with me, and again and again, day after day, I put my hand into myself and find nothing.

Only when I have reached the very edge of bankruptcy, and I am starved almost to death, does the magic purse of myself fill again with its mysterious currency, and from the very brink of my death, like a starved and beaten outcast who has received alms, I buy myself back into life again.

Can I under these circumstances take any credit for my work?

Is this what it is to be an artist?

Sometimes I am so close to the spring of my existence, that I am persuaded by the very constancy of its flow, into the belief that it will never stop.

> Myself, the outcast, has grown many hands
> With which to beg,
> As he begins the pilgrimage into his magic self;
> From which perhaps
> He will never receive the necessary currency
> To pay for his return.